Larry Burkett's

How our House Works

written by Ed Strauss

illustrated by Ed Letwenko

Faith KiDs®
Equipping Kids for Life
faithkids.com

Faith Parenting Guide
Ages 7 and up
Stewardship

Faith Parenting Guide
on page 32.

Faith Kids® is an imprint of Cook Communications Ministries,
Colorado Springs, Colorado 80918
Cook Communications, Paris, Ontario
Kingsway Communications, Eastbourne, England

HOW OUR HOUSE WORKS

First printing, 2002
Printed in the Singapore
1 2 3 4 5 6 7 8 9 10 Printing/Year 06 05 04 03 02

Executive Producer: Allen Burkett
Concept and Direction: Rick Osborne
Editor: Heather Gemmen
Designer: Keith Sherrer, iDesignEtc.

Library of Congress Cataloging-in-Publication Data

Burkett, Larry.
    How our house works / Larry Burkett; illustrator
  Ed Letwenko.
        p. cm. -- (Larry Burkett's how things work)
    Summary: A look at the construction, electrical, plumbing,
  and heating systems of a house, as well as household fur-
  nishings, methods of cleaning, communications equipment,
  and yard care.
    ISBN 0-78143-723-7 (picture book)
      1. Buildings--Mechanical equipment--Juvenile
  literature. 2. Dwellings--Maintenance and
  repair--Juvenile literature. 3. Housekeeping--Juvenile
  literature. [1. Dwellings--Design and construction.
  2. Dwellings--Maintenance and repair. 3. Housekeeping.]
  I. Letwenko, Ed, ill. II. Title.

TH6010 .B87 2002
643--dc21
                                    2001040251

Andy Mann

HI! MY NAME'S ANDY MANN and I build houses right.

I build homes for a living. I'm the foreman on site.

I dig basements, pour concrete, build frameworks and floors.

I oversee workers who walk through the doors.

Now, want some adventure? Let's visit my friends.

You'll learn how homes work. Come on, let's begin. ⚙

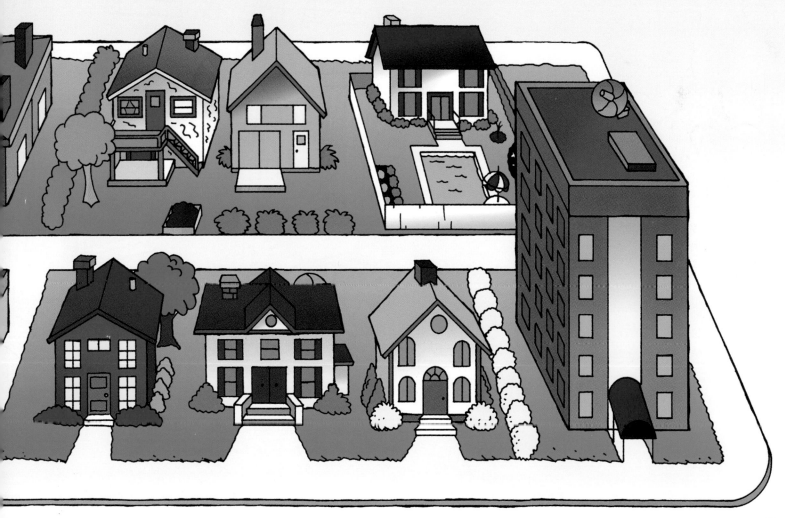

Structural Systems

LET ME TELL YOU HOW my home is built to last long,
Let's look at the framework that's sturdy and strong.
Squinch up your eyes and look straight through my walls;
I'll explain how it's built from the floors to the halls.

Home-building costs money! Big bucks! Understand?
Most homes cost fifty to two hundred grand.
Don't have that much money? Don't lay down and moan.
Your parents have a mortgage:
    that's a giant bank loan.
Each month they make payments
    of hundreds of dollars,
But each year that they pay,
    the mortgage gets smaller. ✿

STUDS: I attach studs to the ceiling boards a couple ways. One is to drive nails in at an angle. The other is to nail them together with metal connectors.

FIRE BLOCKS: I put two-by-four blocking between the studs. If there was a fire, these would block the blaze from spreading rapidly inside the hollow walls.

BRICKS: Here we see a wall made out of bricks. The bricks are held together with mortar.

WALLS: I attach gypsum wallboard to the wall studs with screws, then patch up all the holes.

CONCRETE: The basement and the foundation for the walls are made out of concrete.

5

Electrical Systems

When the Judds' house was built, electricians installed
Electrical wires up and down in the walls.
Some wires lead to switches that flick on the lights,
So Kelly, smart Kelly, can do homework at night.

Each month a man comes, gives their meter a look,
And writes down the numbers with a pen in his book;
And then the bill comes every month in the mail,
Through earthquakes and blizzards,
    the bills never fail.
Sometimes the electric bill gives the Judds jolts,
'Cause they always must pay when they use
    up the volts. ✿

POWER PLANT:
A power plant
in town sends
power to homes
through cables.

**ELECTRICAL
METER:** This meter
keeps track of the electricity that
goes into the house and is used.

WALL PLUGS: Here are electrical wires connected to a receptacle, also known as an electrical outlet or wall plug.

STRINGING WIRE: Wires should be strung through holes drilled in the center of the joists, not strung around the edges.

CIRCUIT BREAKER PANEL (with breaker switches): If there is a power surge and the lights go out, Tom flips the switch to bring the power back on.

Plumbing Systems

Scott and Mary McDuff have children to no end:
Ann, Peter, Bill, Sally, Josh, Ruthie, and Ben.
They like to take baths, and they drink lots of water;
They like to stay clean; so does their pet otter.
So let's stare through their walls, though the effort is numbing,
And get a good look at their pipes and their plumbing.

The meter in the basement keeps ticking *chink-chink*,
When the water's left running in the kitchen sink,
When the dishes are washed, when the clothes get a scrub,
When Ann showers for an hour in the big, big bathtub.
Water might seem cheap, but the stuff isn't free!
For each gallon they guzzle,
    they must pay a fee. ⚙

WATER METER: All water entering the McDuffs' house
passes through the water meter, which measures it.
The main shutoff valve is beside it, in case there is a leak
and all the water needs to be turned off.

DRAIN TRAP: Traps under sinks allow water to drain out, but prevent sewer gas from coming up the drain.

FIRE SPRINKLER: This fire alarm sprinkler is on the kitchen ceiling. If there was a fire, the sprinkler would come on and put it out.

WATER FIXTURES: Hot and cold water is piped to water fixtures throughout the house. Most sinks have hot and cold water faucets. The toilet gets only cold water.

9

Drainage Systems

Now meet the Ho family: dad (Jack) and mom (Jenny);
And their three smart kids: Susan, Lisa, and Kennie;
And five of their schoolmates, who've come for the day:
Mei Li, Joe, Tommy, Big Tony, and Kay.
Let's stare through their walls and peek at their plumbing,
See where water goes when it's all finished coming.

Since we care for God's world, we should try never to pour
Gas or oil or chemicals down drains in the floor.
God made this world beautiful—earth, sky, and streams.
Do your part. Don't pollute. Keep this green planet clean. ⚙

SEPTIC TANKS: Some homes are not connected to a city sewage system. Waste water goes into a septic tank underground, and a special truck comes and empties the tank when it's full.

FLOOR DRAIN: Gravity pulls water down shower drains and drains in basement floors. The waste water goes into the sewer line away from the house.

GUTTERS & DOWN-PIPES: The rain runs down the slanted roof into the gutters, into the downpipe, out the spout at the bottom, and into a drain... which carries rain water away from the house.

11

Climate Control Systems

Now let's visit the Navidads and see how they do:
We'll meet Miguel, Martina, Pedro, and Sara too.
What do they do to stay cool when it's hot?
What do they do to stay warm when it's not? ☀

ANOTHER WINDOW: Since single-pane windows let too much heat pass through, theirs all have double panes. They keep the blinds down too. In the winter, the double panes keep out the cold air.

WINDOWS: When there is a breeze, they open their windows so they won't have to spend money to run the air conditioner. Screens keep out mosquitoes and other bugs.

THERMOSTAT: A thermostat is like a thermometer. The dial is set to a certain point and when the temperature drops below that point, the thermostat makes the furnace go on, heating the house again.

FURNACES: Some furnaces run on electricity. Most run on gas. The flame heats up the air and blows it throughout the house.

FIBERGLASS INSULATION:
Blankets of fiberglass don't let heat or cold pass through very well. This keeps the cold from coming in or the heat from going out.

PEOPLE:
They wear T-shirts to help keep cool in the summer. They dress up wooly warm before they raise the heat in the winter.

FIREPLACE:
During cold months they can help keep the house warm by lighting a fire.

HEAT VENTS:
Here is a heat vent (with the knob turned "open") sending hot air into a room.

AIR CONDITIONER:
This is a the air conditioner, cooling the air and circulating it throughout the house.

13

Furniture Systems

Imagine a house without a bed, table, or chair,

Just a house with walls and floors and lots and lots of air.

Imagine no sofas or desks, nothing but nothing there,

A house that is like a cave for a hibernating bear.

Let's stare through the walls of the Judds' house once more,

And study the furniture that fills up their floors.

Some furniture they really need, some they just desire.

(The price of desirable things is always somewhat higher.)

Even though Laura has arranged her living
    room so nice,

The furniture she filled it with came at
    a modest price.

And that cabinet for the china?

    That fountain for the yard?

Laura used cash, not her credit card. ✿

WHEN THE JUDDS WANT FURNITURE or other expensive items, they save money every month in a savings account. They only buy the items when they have the money saved up.

THE JUDDS SPEND ONLY A CERTAIN AMOUNT of money on entertainment and recreation each month. Not one penny more.

Maintenance Systems

Maintenance means keeping your home running well.
It means taking care of the place where you dwell.
It's all about stewardship, taking care of God's things,
The belongings God gives us, from houses to strings.
So let's look through the walls at the clan of McDuff,
Who are taking time out to take care of their stuff.

Fixing homes costs money. Homes take time to maintain,
But if you don't do the job, the bill will be a huge pain.
So the McDuffs spend a lot at the Home Fixit Store,
Because hiring a repairman costs quite a bit more.
They try not to break things, yes, they treat things with care.
They keep maintenance bills down—
        which are really quite rare. ✿

SANDING WOOD:
Bill is using an
electrical sander to
remove paint off a
wooden rail.

PLUMBING JOBS: This sink only needed a new washer. Peter was able to fix it with his wrench. For more complicated jobs, a professional plumber must be called in.

MASKING WALLS: Before painting, Josh taped wide green tape to the baseboards then put a dropcloth over the floor to keep paint from splattering down the walls onto the baseboards or carpet.

17

Cleanup Systems

Let's go back to the Ho family, dad (Jack) and mom (Jenny),
And their hard-working kids, Susan, Lisa, and Kennie.
Each one plays a part, does a job, does the chores,
Whether scouring the bathtub or scrubbing the floors.

If the toilet stayed grungy, if the deck wasn't mopped,
If the grease wasn't wiped from the places it slopped,
It would take weeks to clean up the grunge;
They'd have to clean with a shovel, not just a sponge.
It's much easier to keep a home clean as one goes;
That's the way things are done at the home of the Hos. ✿

CLEANSERS: Be very careful with cleansers. Don't touch them without your parents knowing. Only adults should use very strong cleansers.

VACUUM CLEANERS: The engine of the vacuum cleaner creates a strong suction to pick up dirt and crumbs from the carpet.

CHEERFUL ATTITUDE: Nehemiah 4:6 says, "The people worked with all their heart." Having a good attitude and doing your part helps make a house a home.

19

Waste & Recycling Systems

Now, let's visit our friends the Navidads again,
And see how they handle recycling, and then
We'll watch what they do with their garbage and trash,
Their cans and their cardboard, their plastic and glass.

They save plastic bottles and aluminum tins,
And refundable glass, yes, they can drop them in bins
In the Recycling Center, where they get back some cash.
See? Certain containers are not simply trash.
Some glass and some plastics don't earn any money,
But they're still worth recycling,
    'cause waste isn't funny. ✿

BOTTLES, JUGS & TINS: Here are the kind of containers that can be recycled in most cities and town in exchange for cash.

COMPOST: Here's a compost pit with rotting vegetable matter and leaves, covered by dirt (to keep the flies out), covered by another layer of compost, another layer of dirt, etc.

TRASH CAN: Now garbage, like fish heads and light bulbs, should be dumped in the trash can, then tied with a twistie before it can stink.

OTHER CONTAINERS: These are the kind of containers that you don't get cash back for, but which can still be recycled. Playground equipment can be made from recycled plastic.

21

Communication Systems

Dad was watching the news, now he's at a commercial,
Mom's talking on the phone to grandfather Herschel,
Kelly's doing her math with the radio playing,
Bill's listening to CDs and thinking of praying.
Jess is e-mailing a friend in Halifax,
Wels is playing level four of "Far-out Bible Facts."

Each month the phone company sends out a bill.
The more calls the Judds make, the bigger the bill.
And their Internet access to get them online,
Of course, costs them money—they pay for
    their time.
The Judds enjoy all this modern communication,
But they try their best to use
    it in moderation.

RADIO: Radio listening's free. The antenna just picks up radio waves in the air.

PHONE LINES: Phone lines were installed alongside the electrical wires in the walls.

TV: With a cable connection or a satellite dish, the company that provides all the channels sends a bill once a month.

PHONES: The phones plug into outlets known as phone jacks.

Yard Care Systems

Now let's ride a helicopter above the houses and trees,
Let's fly with the birds on the blue balmy breeze,
Till the house and yard of the McDuffs is below us;
We'll hover above them. They have something to show us.
They're doing their yard work as busy as ants,
They're wearing their gloves and their hardy work pants.

Where could Mary be and why won't she work?
There's far too much yard work for her to shirk.
No! Here she comes now with lemonade!
She's sharing the sandwiches that she just made! ☼

GARDEN GLOVES: The McDuffs wear gloves when they do yard work. Gloves protect their hands from thorns and sharp objects buried in the soil.

COMPOST: Josh dumps a pail of rotten fruit in the compost box where it will turn into fertilizer.

HAND SPADE: Ann McDuff is using a small garden spade to dig the earth and plant flowers. Spades and hoes are used to dig up larger amounts of dirt.

SHOVELING SNOW:
It's not winter now, but when winter is here, Peter and Ben take turns clearing snow from the sidewalk and driveway.

Clothing Systems

Now let's head down the street and look in on the Hos
Who spent half the day out shopping for clothes.
For today was the day of a savings extravaganza,
In a clothing store known as the Bargain Bonanza.

Such quality clothes for Susan, Lisa,
and Kennie!
When shopping for bargains, Jenny
saved many pennies. ☼

KEEPING TIDY: Hanging once-used clothes back up saves time. Kennie only has to handle them once. If he drops them on the floor, he has to pick them up later. Or worse yet, they might end up in the laundry when they're still clean.

LAUNDRY BASKET: Jenny never mixes colored clothes with white clothes, as the color dyes might stain the white clothes. Not caring for clothes properly could wreck them. That would not be good stewardship.

CLOSETS: Shirts and pants and dresses should be hung on hangers. Sweaters and T-shirts can be stacked on the shelf above the hanging space.

DONATION BOX: When her kids outgrow clothes, Jenny sorts through them and thinks how to share them.

WASHING MACHINE: Clean clothes shouldn't go in the wash. It costs precious cash to use the washer and dryer, precious hours to iron clothes and fold them.

CLOTHES WASHER AND DRYER: Jenny never puts just two or three items in the wash. That would waste water and power. She always makes sure she has a full load.

Food Systems

The clan of McDuff worked hard all day.

They worked up an appetite that wouldn't go away.

Good thing that Scott went grocery shopping already

And stuck to the list that called for spaghetti.

While they did all their chores, Mary whipped up a dinner:

with salad and garlic bread—oh boy, what a winner! ✿

COUPONS: Here's the supermarket flyer— or what's left of it. Scott ripped out all the money-saving coupons and turned them in to the cashier.

BARGAINS: Scott really knows how to zero in on bargains. By not necessarily picking brand names, he saved a lot of money. He also saved money by checking the receipt. He noticed that the cashier had forgotten to ring in a sale price.

SHOPPING LIST: It's very wise to write up a shopping list ahead of time and to stick to it when shopping. This prevents impulse buying.

Safety Systems

Keeping a home safe is a great thing,
  for sure;
The Judd family's home is safe and secure.
The kids don't leave toys in the stairways
  or halls,
No guest ever trips on lost teddies and balls.
Cleansers and bleach and dangerous
  chemicals
Are kept on a shelf, not in closets where
  Kelly goes.
And watchdogs? Well, they have a collie
  named Spark
Who licks strangers' hands and forgets he
  should bark. ✿

PRAYING: Before sleeping the Judds thank God that his angels will watch over them and their guests that night.

WINDOWS: Tom closes things up for the night: they shut all their shutters and lock windows.

DOORS: Laura bolts all the doors and check all the locks.

SMOKE DETECTOR: This appliance is attached to the ceiling and is designed to detect smoke. This keeps the family safe.

SECURITY ALARM: This security alarm has wires attached to the windows and doors. This protects the house. Also, if anyone walks in front of the motion detector, a light comes on. This keeps strangers away from the house.

PREVENTING FIRES. Most drywall (gypsum board) these days does not burn. Also, the insulation inside the walls is not flammable. This protects the family.

Faith
Parenting
Guide

Ages
7 and up

Stewardship

How Our House Works

Life Issue: I want my children to learn why they should take care of their things.

Help your children learn about stewardship in the following ways:

Sight: Walk through your house together and look for all the ways your home is showing good stewardship: Are lights turned off in empty rooms? Are you recycling? Do you have a compost pile? Are family members dressed properly to keep warm or cool? Are you careful with the water you use? See if you can come up with other ways to be a stewardship family.

Sound: Let your children choose their favorite thanksgiving and worship songs to sing together. After you thank God in song for all the blessings he has given your family, take some time to tell God that you will take care of everything he has given you the very best you can.

Touch: Borrow or purchase the game Money Matters for Kids, pull out the popcorn and milkshakes, and settle down for a family fun night. Don't try to teach your children about stewardship while you play; simply have fun and let the game speak for itself. ✿